Mail Carrier

Laura K. Murray

seedlings

CREATIVE EDUCATION • CREATIVE PAPERBACKS

Published by Creative Education and Creative Paperbacks
P.O. Box 227, Mankato, Minnesota 56002
Creative Education and Creative Paperbacks
are imprints of The Creative Company
www.thecreativecompany.us

Design by Ellen Huber
Production by Grant Gould
Art direction by Rita Marshall
Printed in the United States of America

Photographs by Alamy (ClassicStock, Keith Homan, ZUMA Press Inc), Getty (Design Pics, Dann Tardif), iStockphoto (allanswart, Allkindza, Lana2011, LPETTET, solidcolours, xxmmxx, Drazen Zigic), Shutterstock (eddtoro, Fototocam, Pixel-Shot, Andrey_Popov, Drazen Zigic)

Copyright © 2023 Creative Education, Creative Paperbacks
International copyright reserved in all countries.
No part of this book may be reproduced in any form without written permission from the publisher.

ISBN 9781640264137 (library binding)
ISBN 9781628329469 (paperback)
ISBN 9781640005778 (eBook)

LCCN 2020907030

TABLE OF CONTENTS

Hello, Mail Carriers! 5

Delivering Mail 6

City and Country 9

Driving and Walking 10

All Kinds of Weather 12

A Mail Carrier's Gear 14

What Do Mail Carriers Do? 16

Thank You, Mail Carriers! 18

Picture a Mail Carrier 20

Words to Know 22

Read More 23

Websites 23

Index 24

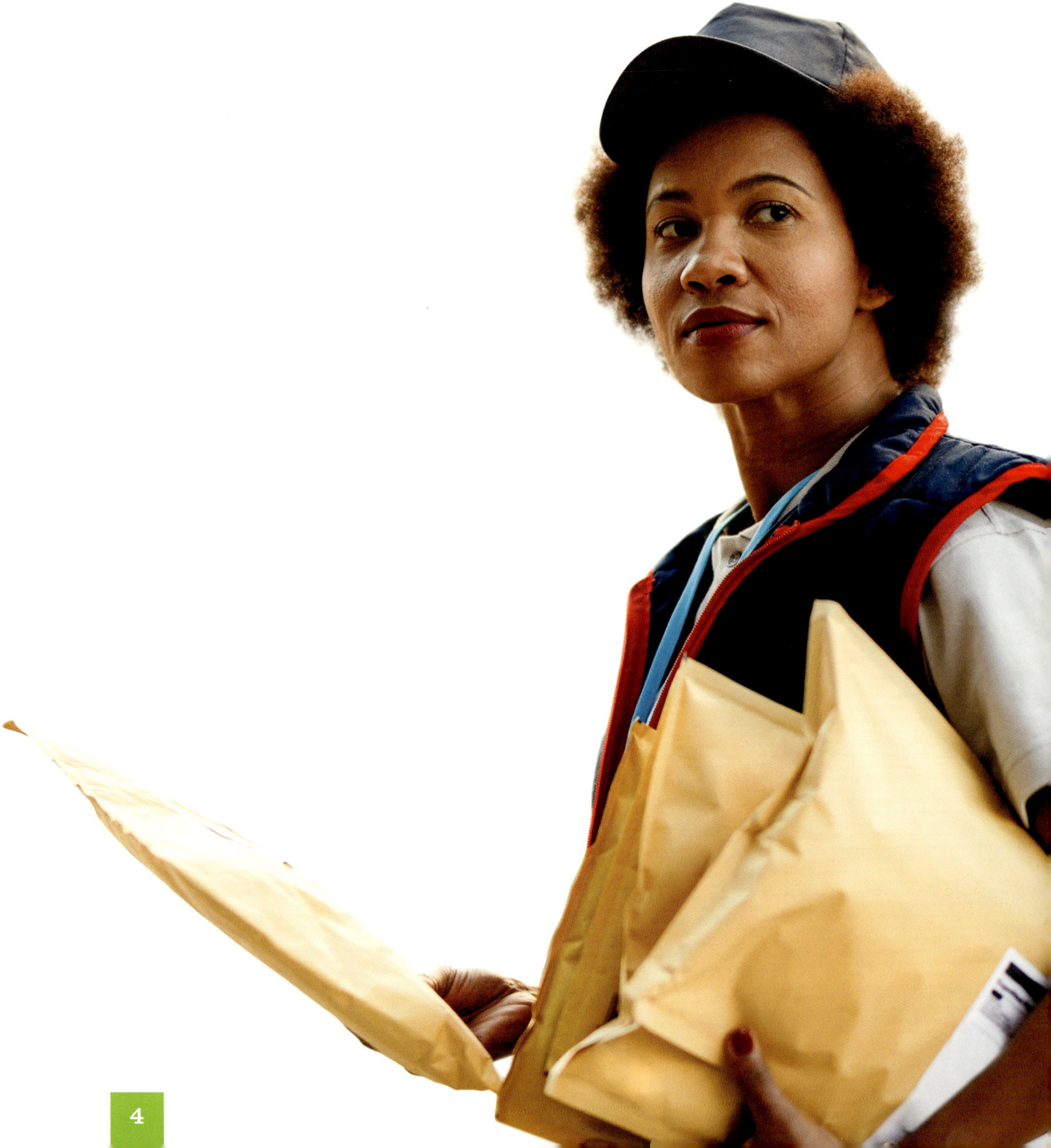

Hello,
mail carriers!

Mail carriers deliver mail.

They take care of letters and **packages**.

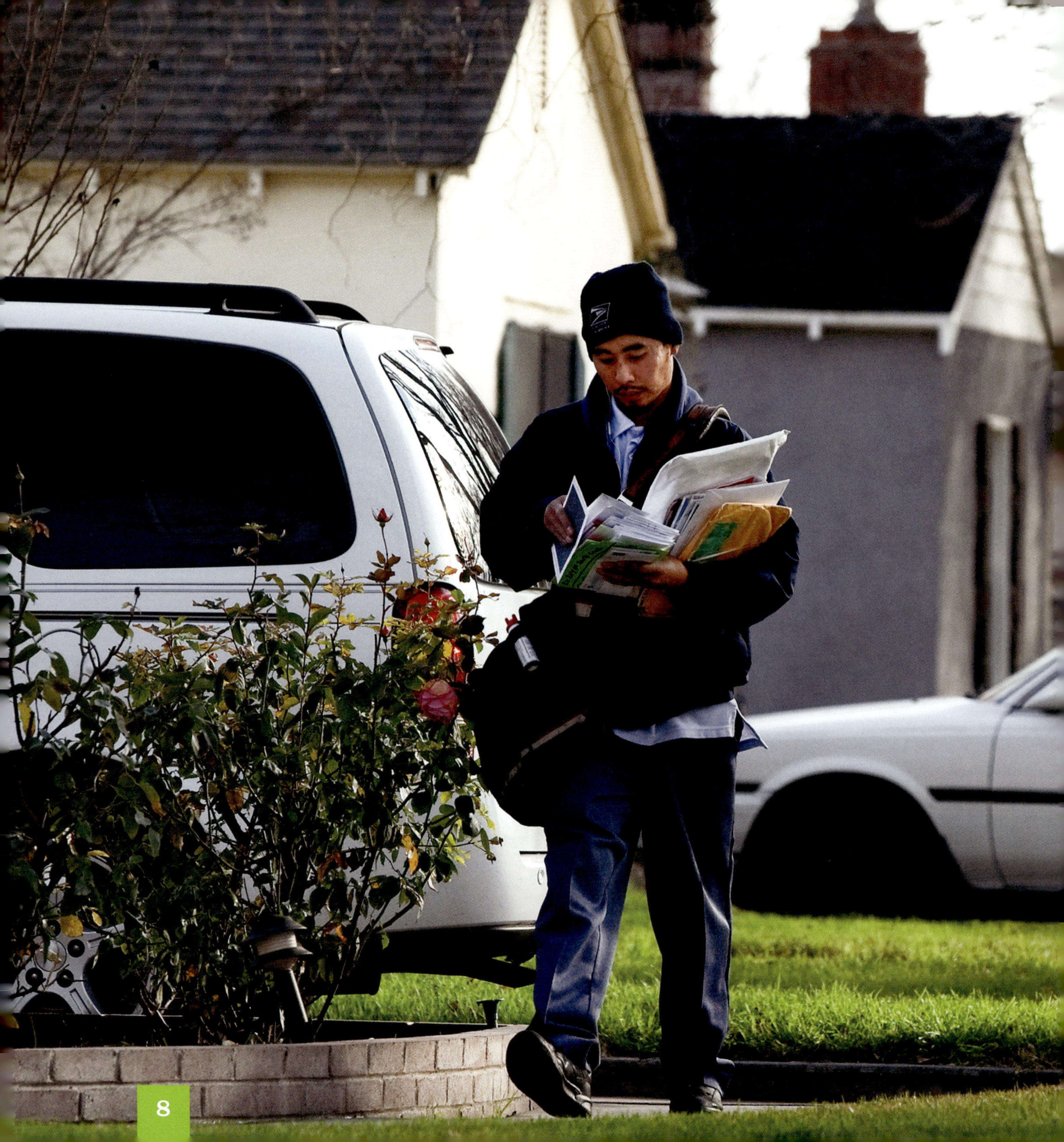

Mail carriers work for the post office. They work in towns. They work in rural areas, too.

Some mail carriers drive a truck.

Others walk. They carry mail in a bag. It can be heavy!

Mail carriers work in any weather. They work in heat and cold. They work in snow and rain.

13

Mail carriers wear good walking shoes.

They need warm clothes for winter. A hat blocks the sun.

Mail carriers pick up mail.

16

They sort it.
They put letters in mailboxes.

17

Thank you,

mail carriers!

Picture a Mail Carrier

hat

vest

package

20

mailbox

letter

mail bag

Words to Know

packages: boxes or things that are wrapped

post office: the place in charge of the mail

rural: areas outside of towns or cities

sort: to put into groups

Read More

Devera, Czeena. *Mail Carrier.*
Ann Arbor, Mich.: Cherry Lake Publishing, 2018.

Leaf, Christina. *Mail Carriers.*
Minneapolis: Bellwether Media, 2018.

Websites

Mail Carrier Coloring Page
http://www.supercoloring.com/coloring-pages/mail-carrier

Post Office Video
https://pbs.org/video/kidvision-vpk-youve-got-mail

Note: Every effort has been made to ensure that the websites listed above are suitable for children, that they have educational value, and that they contain no inappropriate material. However, because of the nature of the Internet, it is impossible to guarantee that these sites will remain active indefinitely or that their contents will not be altered.

bag 11
clothes 14, 15
letters 7, 17
mail 6, 11, 16
mailboxes 17
packages 7
post office 9
truck 10
weather 12, 15
work areas 9